YOUR KNOWLEDGE HAS VALUE

AF149256

- We will publish your bachelor's and master's thesis, essays and papers

- Your own eBook and book - sold worldwide in all relevant shops

- Earn money with each sale

Upload your text at www.GRIN.com and publish for free

Bibliographic information published by the German National Library:

The German National Library lists this publication in the National Bibliography; detailed bibliographic data are available on the Internet at http://dnb.dnb.de .

Imprint:

Copyright © 2015 GRIN Verlag, Open Publishing GmbH
Print and binding: Books on Demand GmbH, Norderstedt Germany
ISBN: 9783668224940

This book at GRIN:

http://www.grin.com/en/e-book/323334/the-main-effects-of-globalisation-on-the-economic-social-and-political

William Garner

The main effects of globalisation on the economic, social and political developments in Latin America

GRIN Publishing

GRIN - Your knowledge has value

Since its foundation in 1998, GRIN has specialized in publishing academic texts by students, college teachers and other academics as e-book and printed book. The website www.grin.com is an ideal platform for presenting term papers, final papers, scientific essays, dissertations and specialist books.

Visit us on the internet:

http://www.grin.com/

http://www.facebook.com/grincom

http://www.twitter.com/grin_com

What have been the main effects of globalisation on economic/social/political development? Answer with reference to either Latin America or Africa

Firstly to understand the effects of globalisation, it is important to define globalisation beforehand. Globalisation is a difficult term to be defined in a simple sentence however can be agreed it is an increase in interconnectedness between countries around the globe in terms of trade, travel, financial markets and institutions and areas such as tourism. Mullard and Cole (2007) defines globalisation as "Within this context globalisation is defined in terms of the compressing and the stretching of geographical spaces, where technology, information exchanges, the knowledge economy…this form of globalisation is to be celebrated because it confirms the ascendancy of competitive markets, the expansion of free trade, and the break-up of monopolies and protectionist policies." This confirms, that although it is difficult to define globalisation as it lacks an agreed definition, it all expands around the increased interconnectedness of nations around the globe. In regards to Latin America globalisation has a number of reasons to affect the development of the economic, social and political aspect of the landscape. Key economic effects that need to be expanded on includes the impact of trade in terms of Gross Domestic Product and the Balance of Payments through imports and exports and also the potential benefit of investment opportunities in South America through globalisation. Social impacts that need to be expanded upon include poverty and crime and the politics behind working conditions and regulations. Politically, governments have been able to communicate more effectively allowing for support between nations, trade pacts and negotiations, while also discussing the neo-liberalist push for Latin America to adopt the Washington Consensus. These key areas need to be discussed more closely, in particularly the negative effects that these can cause and in terms of South America, the exploitation that has been quite common since the growth of globalisation.

Economically, globalisation has had a major impact on Latin America for better and for worse. The spread of neoliberalism in the 1990s has allowed the influx of transnational corporations (TNCs) in Latin America. This US led programme pushed for privatisation of industries and the growth of enterprise and free-market values allowing for TNCs to take advantage of low national wages and new markets in areas such as Latin America. According to Greer and Singh (2000) that in the 20th century: "National expansion by companies almost exclusively from the United States and a handful of Western European Nations Sixty per cent of these corporations' investments went to Latin America, Asia, Africa, and the Middle East. Fuelled by numerous mergers and acquisitions, monopolistic and oligopolistic concentration of large transnationals in major sectors such as petrochemicals and food also had its roots in these years." The methods of TNCs allowed them to expand through both vertical integration and horizontal integration into growing markets in Latin America maintaining monopolistic markets with few major competitors particularly in recently privatised industries. Although there are concerns of too many negative economic externalities of globalisation in Latin America as mentioned in regards to exploitation. However, it cannot be misinterpreted in that there are clear benefits to the economies of Latin America through globalisation. A good example of this is Venezuela which has had large oil deposits. Through this Venezuela has had access to the global oil market and thereby benefited from large export-led growth which according to the theory on aggregate demand leads to economic growth as exports allow liquidity (money) to enter Venezuela's circular flow of income. Figure 1.1 shows the impact of increased exports affecting the aggregate demand curve. The increase in exports causes aggregate demand if all else is the same up along the aggregate supply curve from (P, Y) to (P1, Y1) shifting aggregate demand up the curve from (AD) to (AD1). This increases the price level from (P) to (P1) and the output/national income to rise from (Y) to (Y1). The equilibrium will therefore also rise to (P1) (Y1) from (P) (Y) along the aggregate supply curve shown in the figure. This should allow for an increase in wages and economic growth. Jobs are also created by the oil industry and also businesses investing in Latin America through globalisation, this leads to the multiplier effect as those employed will spend disposable income in shops which not only increases economic growth but also means businesses will hire more staff and new businesses will be created to meet demand. This in term causes more employment and so on, benefiting the economy and increasing employment in Latin America. Despite criticisms that large amounts of employment to TNCs are exploitive such as mining resources and factory work such as sweat shops. Ellwood (2001) states that TNCs become the "dominant economic player, creating jobs (albeit fewer of them) and boosting national incomes". Lodge and Wilson (2006) partially agree with and argue that "Multinational corporations create jobs, bring access to credit and markets, introduce new technologies, often reduce the prices of goods and services, and increase the wealth of the host economy through payments of taxes and wage income. MNCs also, on average, pay higher wages than domestic companies." This shows that although Lodge and Wilson agree with Ellwood on the increase of income due to MNCs and TNCs, however, Lodge and Wilson differ in opinion in contending that the economy is strengthened along with an increase to wealth and potential jobs which is surely better than being unemployed and in absolute poverty. This could be more of a political issue due to the lack of regulations on health and safety and working conditions in Latin America while there is also a lot of evidence suggesting corruption, however, this political issue will be discussed later. One of the main issues, is that Latin America is focusing too heavily on exports to boost economic growth through its global connections. The Economist (2014) states in regards to Latin America that "The growing trade gap has given rise to two worries: that the region is relying too heavily on basic exports again and succumbing to a "natural-resource curse", as it has done before; and that it will take the wrong lesson from China and embrace state capitalism." This demonstrates that globalisation has benefited Latin America through potential trade routes and markets to sell its products. By following the example of China through mainly focusing on export-led growth through using large MNCs and TNCs has yielded results on the one hand such as through economic growth and increased employment, but on the other hand it has caused economic issues such as high inflation. According to Cawthorne and Ore (2014) Venezuela's: "12-month inflation, which is the highest in the Americas, reached 63.6 percent in November." This growing threat of inflation weakens the currency of an economy while the instability it is likely to cause on the economy and consumer confidence as well as foreign direct investment (FDI) influxes is problematic.

The shadow economy is a significant indicator of an unstable economy. In Latin America, the shadow economy contains a large chunk of total percent of national income in Latin America. Schneider and Williams' (2013) chart as shown in figure 1.2, illustrates "The Shadow Economy % of National Income 2007". In the case of Latin America, countries such as Argentina had 25.3% of National Income is through the Shadow Economy. Venezuela had even higher at 33.8% while Bolivia being the highest at 66.1%. This is in comparison with the USA at 8.6% and Canada at 15.3%.

This denotes that many of the countries in Latin America have a large shadow economy where goods and services are traded illegally and without taxation. The effect of globalisation on opening markets to new goods and services means that Latin American has a market for imports, however, due to a weak currency as the economy is quite unstable because of high, varied inflation. The impact of this is a lack of FDI and a reduced value in the currencies in South America. This means that many imports may be bought illegally to be more affordable. Another knock on effect of this is that the government get less revenue and thereby are likely to struggle to fund infrastructure, welfare and other amenities to increase confidence and reduce poverty and economic instability. Coyle (1998) States that "when the criminal element grows too large it eats the foundations of the bulk of the economy from within. It is growing alarmingly now, exploiting more efficiently than any multinational the opportunities afforded by globalisation." This confirms that this is prevalent in Latin America that contains large numbers of illegal markets start to take over the economy as agreed upon with figure 1.2 and the out of control shadow economy. This is not going to boost the economy as efficiently that the usual means such as through the private sector multiplier effect and government spending for public services which is funded through the growth of businesses and consumers. Arvate et al. (2005) state that: "An increase of the shadow economy can lead to reduced state revenues which in turn reduce the quality and quantity of publicly provided goods and services." The impact of this is dramatic on the economy potentially damaging it and allowing illegal trades to get out of control.

Politically, globalisation has had a fair impact on Latin America. Dating all the way back to the slave trade and political involvement in areas such as the sugar trade all the way to the current oil and coffee industries to benefit the economies and infrastructure of countries in Latin America. This meant that the political system was developed significantly through globalisation and the influence of other trading partners and governments. The United States' liberalisation programme on nations in Latin America involved a large amount of governments who expanded on free-market ideologies and further access to the world market and reduced protectionist policies. Rodrik (2006) states that "Stabilize, privatize and liberalize" became the mantra of a generation of technocrats who cut their teeth in the developing world and of the political leaders they counselled." Also the growth of the private sector through being encouraged to privatise industries allowing MNCs and TNCs access to new markets.

One of the main political issues in relation to Latin America is corruption. Kurczy (2013) states that "Latin American nations are more interested in justifying corruption that in tackling the problem." This is rife due to the impact of a more open market with not enough enforcement and regulations while still maintaining a large public sector vulnerable to bribery and not as efficient as private businesses which had been crowded-out. This means businesses, whose primary objectives include profit maximisation will try and increase its profits anyway it can essentially legally although some businesses and individuals may take this further if there is opportunity to do so. Friedman (1976) stated that: "some government officials (who, after all, spend other people's money) are tempted to use their position for personal gain, that private enterprises are tempted to accommodate them, and that those enterprises that resist the temptation may well lose profitable business." This is problematic for large governments in Latin America as organised crime and the drug trade can flourish through bribing officials essentially allowing the shadow economy to grow and thereby lead to government failure due to the involvements of the public sector. The political system has some clear flaws due to globalisation, however, with the correct leadership and further efforts to reduce corruption, Latin America could potentially sort out its political issues.

There are many social effects of globalisation. The Washington Consensus that pushed out neo-liberalist policies from the US to countries in Latin America was much more intense form of globalisation that the past .This allowed Latin America to gain large economic benefits, although some serious social implications, (Bray and Woodford 1999) expand on this in regards to the Neo-liberalist push of globalisation upon Latin America and the social impact: "The consequences of neoliberalist policies are far reaching for any nation, but particularly hurtful for the majority of Latin American residents. Income inequality has increased in most nations that have implemented the reforms". This stresses that due to the impacts of the Washington Consensus on Latin America meant inequality has become a major social problem. Evidence obtained by (Cooper and Heine 2009) partially agrees and disagrees with Bray and Woodford stating that "Poverty, however, did go down: affecting 46 per cent of the populations of 18 countries in 1990, the poverty rate fell to 41.8 per cent between 1998 and 2001." This shows that poverty did actually fall, however, this could be due to big poverty reduction schemes by government in Mexico, Brazil and Chile. They go on to state: "Yet the absolute number of Latin Americans below the poverty line went up in those years, from 190 million in 1990 to 209 million in 2001." This means that although the poverty percentage fell, the number of people that are in poverty actually rose.

The Human Development Index (HDI) is a system that is used to measure countries' education, life expectancy and income indices and puts the countries in four tiers. Figure 1.3 shows the HDI of the global map including Latin America. The HDI map shows that Latin America has mostly "high" and "very high" human development. This expresses that there may be some poverty, although, the indices show that there is a high or very high life expectancy, educational system and income in regards to countries that have been indexed. This disagrees in that there is less poverty than there is made out to be while the education system may be a key long-term prospect for the development of Latin America through allowing the public to be educated and prevent future crime and poverty. Payne (2011) states that: "I shall also list some of the remedies attempted at reducing crime, and its' source poverty, with a focus on the only true answer for both problems: education." This in turn shows that the potential of the growing HDI indices particularly a rise in education could lead to the reduction of crime and the size of the shadow economy while also reducing future poverty. This underlines the fact that globalisation may in the long-run reduce poverty and crime and improve some of the social issues especially through the correct government involvement such as through welfare and minimum wage policies.

The weight of the evidence indicates that globalisation has had a huge impact on Latin America through both positive and negative effects on economic, political and the social position of countries in Latin America. The major effects of globalisation on Latin America includes significant economic benefits through trade and the ability for Latin America to have access to the global market allowing economic growth through exports. The initial implications of globalisation to Latin America seems to impact the population through very low wages for labour and poor working conditions, however, this could be down to corruption and a lack of health and safety regulations from government. Also the fact that government has grown too large and crowded out private businesses meant that there is easy access for bribery and corruption while government figures may be less keen to regulate and push for decent wages. To remedy this continuation of policies such as increased funding of education to reduce poverty and crime and allow the reduction in the shadow economy and a growth of enterprise and economic growth. If the correct conditions are met in the form of political policies and a reduced, less corruptible government to allow Latin America enterprises, businesses and the economy to reap the rewards of access to a global market and the potential to reduce some of the negative externalities of globalisation such as crime and poverty.

Appendices

Figure 1.1: Revision Guru (2015). *Aggregate Demand.* Available: http://revisionguru.co.uk/revisionguru/economics-2/economics-as-unit-2/aggregate-demand/. Last accessed 25th February 2014.

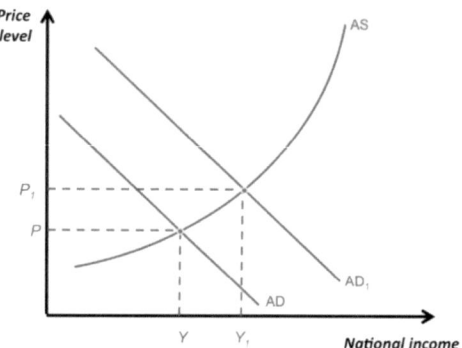

Figure 1.2: World Economics (2015). *The Shadow Economy % of National Income 2007.* Available: http://www.worldeconomics.com/Papers/Measuring%20The%20Americas%20GDP_7fbab7d6-44fd-4f40-b4bb-233fb5aeaab5.paper. Last accessed 25th February 2015.

Country	% of National Income
USA	8.6
Canada	15.3
Chile	19.3
Argentina	25.3
Costa Rica	25.7
Mexico	30
Dominican Republic	30.5
Trinidad & Tobago	31.5
Ecuador	32.4
Venezuela	33.8
Jamaica	34.8
Colombia	37.3
Paraguay	37.4
Brazil	39
Nicaragua	43.1
El Salvador	45.1
Guatemala	50.5
Honduras	48.3
Uruguay	50.6
Peru	58
Panama	60
Bolivia	66.1
Average	**36.9**

Source: Schneider and Williams (2013)

Figure 1.3: Human Development Index (2014). *UN Human Development Index 2014 – Latin American Perspectives.* Available: https://eyeonlatinamerica.wordpress.com/2014/08/12/un-hdi-2014-latin-america/. Last accessed 6th March 2015.

"Global map showing the levels of human development according to the 2014 HDI (with dark blue showing Very High Human Development, blue showing High, light blue showing Medium, and pale showing Low)".

Bibliography

Arvate, P., Ribeiro de Lucinda, C. and Schneider, F. (2005). *Shadow Economies In Latin America: What Do We Know? A Highlight On Brazil*. Ph.D. São Paulo.

Bray, Marjorie Woodford. (1999). Trade As an Instrument of Dominance: The Latin American Experience. Latin American Perspectives, 26(5), 55-75.

Cawthorne, A. and Ore, D. (2015). *UPDATE 1-Venezuela confirms recession, inflation hits 63.6 percent in Nov*. [online] Reuters. Available at: http://www.reuters.com/article/2014/12/30/venezuela-economy-idUSL1N0UE1FY20141230 [Accessed 27 Feb. 2015].

Cooper, A. and Heine, J. (2009). *Which way Latin America?* Tokyo: United Nations University Press, p.8.

Coyle, D. (1998). *The dark side of globalisation where the black economy thrives*. [online] The Independent. Available at: http://www.independent.co.uk/news/business/the-dark-side-of-globalisation-where-the-black-economy-thrives-1159998.html [Accessed 11 Feb. 2015].

Ellwood, W. (2001). *The no-nonsense guide to globalization*. Oxford, England: New Internationalist, p.57.

Friedman, M. (1976). "The Uses of Corruption". *Newsweek*, p.73.

Greer, J. and Singh, K. (2000). *A Brief History of Transnational Corporations*. [online] Globalpolicy.org. Available at: https://www.globalpolicy.org/empire/47068-a-brief-history-of-transnational-corporations.html [Accessed 10 Feb. 2015].

Kurczy, S. (2013). *Global corruption: How does Latin America stack up?*. Available: http://www.csmonitor.com/World/Americas/Latin-America-Monitor/2013/1203/Global-corruption-How-does-Latin-America-stack-up. Last accessed 7th March 2015.

Lodge, G. and Wilson, C. (2006). *A corporate solution to global poverty*. Princeton, N.J.: Princeton University Press, p.11.

Mullard, M, Bankole, C. (2007). *Globalisation, Citizenship and the War on Terror.* Cheltenham: Edward Elgar Publishing Limited. 83.

Payne, M. (2011) *Crime and Poverty.* Arizona: Arizona University Press, p.2

Rodrik, D. (2006). Goodbye Washington Consensus, Hello Washington Confusion? *Journal of Economic Literature*, 1(1), pp.1, 2.

Stephen, K. (2013). *Global corruption: How does Latin America stack up?* [online] The Christian Science Monitor. Available at: http://www.csmonitor.com/World/Americas/Latin-America-Monitor/2013/1203/Global-corruption-How-does-Latin-America-stack-up [Accessed 27 Feb. 2015].

The Economist (2015) Pacific Pumas. *The Economist*, pp.13-14.

Tradingeconomics.com, (2015). *Venezuela Unemployment Rate | 1999-2015 | Data | Chart | Calendar.* [online] Available at: http://www.tradingeconomics.com/venezuela/unemployment-rate [Accessed 15 Feb. 2015].

YOUR KNOWLEDGE HAS VALUE